FINDING TRUE HAPPINESS

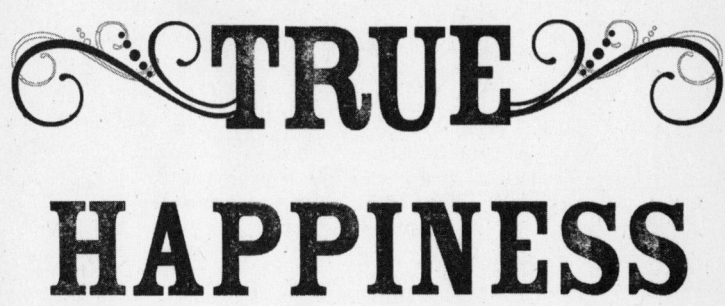

FULTON SHEEN

DynamicCatholic.com

Be Bold. Be Catholic®

TABLE OF CONTENTS

This book is dedicated to
St. John Neumann, America's first
--but probably not her last--
canonized bishop.

Introduction

Archbishop Fulton Sheen rescued me from misery when I was in college. I had been operating under the common misconception that happiness was to be found in possessing certain external things. When I failed to obtain those things, I was miserable. My happiness had been held back from me, I thought. Those things I had been so intent on obtaining--whether a grade in a class, a particular job, or a friendship--had power over me. What was I to do?

Archbishop Sheen told me just what to do through his writings. The first was to let go of the idea that happiness is to be found in things outside oneself. Happiness does not depend on accumulating more things, but on the mindset we have concerning the things we already do possess. Happiness does not consist in having more, but in appreciating more. As Sheen wrote, "It is not so much what happens in your life that matters; it is rather how you react to it."

We oftentimes don't have direct control over external things, but we do have control over our internal view of those things. What is important is not getting an external result, but putting our best effort forth in trying to do something good. "The talents we have must be put to work, but if they yield only a certain return, we do not murmur because the return is not greater," the great archbishop explained.

It's not a matter of sloth, but of reasonable desires. We don't expect what cannot be given, whether from an inherent possibility (getting water from a book) or from a particular situation (another baseball team playing better than our team on a given day). We'll never get a drink from a book, but tomorrow our team may get a win over the team that beats us today.

The most important battle, however, is not external. It is the one that occurs in the soul.

"He who does not find the enemy within will find the enemy without," Sheen stated. He said everyone has a "civil war" going on inside between the higher and lower self, but if the reality of this war is not accepted, we will end up bringing that war into the lives of those around us. "The choice is between engaging in a battle within, or a battle without. If we don't combat our own selfishness, we will selfishly combat other people."

It may seem at first glance that by simply opting out of the internal war, we can make everything okay. However, denying our selfishness doesn't work. Doing so will only make us more selfish, and thus, more miserable. By contrast, when we admit our need for self-denial, we will be able to enjoy peace--a peace that emanates from the inside out. This brings us to a beautiful paradox regarding the very name, *Fulton Sheen*. In Gaelic, "fulton" means "war" and "sheen" means "peace." In one person, there are two distinct names, and peace comes after (internal) war.

Fulton J. Sheen was born in El Paso, Illinois on May 8, 1895, the eldest of Delia and Newton Sheen's four boys. After battling tuberculosis as an infant, he went on to become an excellent student. High school valedictorian honors were followed by degrees from St. Viator College in Illinois and St. Paul Seminary in Minnesota. After being ordained to the priesthood, Sheen pursued more degrees from The Catholic University of America in Washington, D.C., and the University of Louvain in Belgium. He then became the first American to earn an *agrege en philosophie*, a so-called "super-doctorate"--and with highest honors at that.

Far from letting so much education prevent him from communicating with the average man, Sheen retained his ability to speak the truth in straightforward terms. Analogies, simple stories, and humor were tools he used to convey profound realities in plain language. His popularity was manifested in the fact that he had over 60 books published on topics ranging from St. Therese of Lisieux to Communism.

In this wide array of subjects, Sheen's most needed and helpful seems to have been finding true happiness. So much sadness was prevalent in his time, which he attributed to increased selfishness and corresponding distance from God. "If you do not worship God, you worship something, and nine times out of ten it will be yourself," he stated bluntly.

"You have a duty to worship God, not because He will be imperfect and unhappy if you do not, but because you will be imperfect and unhappy" if you do not.

By applying this principle to the Soviet Union, Sheen demonstrated the great destruction that atheistic regimes do to the human soul. At a time when some wanted to overlook the evils of Communism, Sheen was presenting them to the American public in books, and on the radio and television. One of the most memorable episodes of his popular television shows was one in which he condemned Communism in dramatic fashion. He said that Joseph Stalin, like every other human being, would one day meet his judgment, and within a week, Stalin did just that, dying on March 5, 1953.

Those souls willing to repent of their errors and surrender to God found a friend in Sheen. One of the most striking examples of this was Bella Dodd, who grew up Catholic but drifted into

Communism. She was a lawyer for the Communist Party in the United States, but became disillusioned with the system she once thought would bring her happiness.

After talking with Sheen about her atheistic political beliefs, she was still reluctant to come back to God. However, after Sheen led her to a nearby chapel and knelt down to pray, Dodd began crying. She had been touched by the grace of God and returned to the Church.

Praying in chapels became second nature to Sheen, as he committed himself early on to a daily Holy Hour. He kept this practice for over 60 years, amidst extraordinary demands on his time, which included travels throughout the world. He called it "the hour that makes my day," and attributed his ability to reach people to this specific practice of prayer. Two months and one week after meeting Pope John Paul II in 1979 at St. Patrick's Cathedral in New York City, Sheen died on December 9 in his chapel before the Blessed Sacrament.

Because Sheen died well over 15 years before my personal discovery of his writings, I received somewhat of a history lesson from his books. I learned about the people he influenced years ago through his highly-rated television and radio shows, extensive missionary work, and of course, his books. I read of how he would receive more letters from non-Catholics than from Catholics, and even won an Emmy for his work.

However, I was unaware of anyone my own age who was acquainted with him. What I grew to realize since then is that Sheen's legacy most certainly did not die with him. His is not a story simply of the past, but also of the present and future, made known though conventional and modern media. Many of his books are still in print, and even more of his recordings are available in various audio and video formats.

Sheen's message also lives on through countless priests who admire not only what he had to say, but how he said it. Indeed, he is commonly regarded as the greatest preacher of the 20th century. However, his influence is perhaps even more noticeable in the laity than in the clergy. Many notable laymen on Catholic radio and television--including Raymond Arroyo of EWTN, Patrick Coffin of Catholic Answers, and Jesse Romero of the Catholic Resource Center--have been inspired by Sheen.

Quite humorously, though, Sheen was not always impressed with himself. He told a story of a man walking into St. Patrick's Cathedral and, not recognizing Sheen, saying he wanted to go to Confession. He had heard Sheen on the radio and sharply criticized him in front of three non-Catholics, saying that "Dr. Fulton Sheen" drove him crazy. Though the man thought he had given scandal, Sheen counseled him not to worry, saying he himself sometimes shared the same opinion of "Dr. Sheen."

It is interesting to note that one of the conditions of happiness, as explained by Sheen in his writings, is not taking oneself too seriously. The more highly we regard ourselves, the more miserable we become; while the more lowly we regard ourselves in the light of God's grace, the more content we become. This is something another American bishop learned decades before Sheen.

St. John Neumann (1811-1860) had many things in common with Sheen, starting with physical appearance. Both had piercing eyes and both were short: Neumann five feet, two inches; Sheen five feet, seven inches. However, the two clergymen made up for their lack of height in energy, dedication, and intellectual capacity. Both had a great love for Jesus in the Blessed Sacrament, and of course, both were bishops.

Neumann, like Sheen, had the ability to convey in clear terms the way to happiness, and this was due in part to his own internal struggles earlier in life. The naturalized American citizen battled depression in his early twenties, feeling as if God had abandoned him.

"Lord, I am beginning to feel that awful state of depression coming over me again! I lose all yearning for prayer because you have seemed to turn a deaf ear to my cries," he lamented.

After straining for consolation, Neumann realized the seeming contradiction of happiness, that you find it by stopping the search for it. He wrote, "I no longer look for comfort from either Heaven or earth. You, Divine Master, can judge whether such are necessary for me. I promise to worry no more over the aridity You send me. You, my God, are the font both of aridity and grace." An act of thanksgiving followed, as did his peace of mind.

Decades later, Sheen would express the same basic concept: "It is one of the paradoxes of creation that you gain control by submission." Only by letting go can we gain real power. As long as we hold onto things, those things have power over us, but if we let go of having things our way, we are freed up to be happy.

In the pages that follow, Sheen--officially declared venerable in 2012--explains in more detail how one can become truly happy. His helpful words are taken from the books: *Walk With God, Way to Happiness, Way to Inner Peace,* and *You.*

–**Trent Beattie**
March 19, 2013, Feast Day of Saint Joseph

FINDING PERFECT HAPPINESS

Are you perfectly happy? Or are you still looking for happiness? There can be no doubt that at one time or another in your life you attained that which you believed would make you happy. When you got what you wanted, were you happy?

Do you remember when you were a child, how ardently you looked forward to Christmas? How happy you thought you would be, with your fill of cakes, your hands glutted with toys, and your eyes dancing with the lights on the tree!

Christmas came, and after you had eaten your fill, blown out the last Christmas candle, and played till your toys no longer amused, you climbed into your bed and said, in your own little heart of hearts, that somehow or other it did not quite come up to your expectations. And have you not lived that experience over a thousand times since?

Perhaps it was marriage you thought which would bring you perfect happiness. Even though it did bring a measure of happiness, you admit that you now take your companion's love for granted. One is never thirsty at the border of the well…

Maybe it was a desire to be well-known that you craved. You did become well-known, only to find that reputation is like a ball; as soon as it starts rolling, men begin to kick it around.

The fact is: you want to be perfectly happy, but you are not. Your life has been a series of disappointments, shocks, and disillusionments. How have you reacted to your disappointments? Either you became cynical or else you became religious. If you became cynical, you blamed things rather than yourself. If you were married, you said: "If I had another husband, or another wife, I would be happy." Or you said: "If I had another job…," or "If I visited another nightclub…," or "If I were in another city, I would be happy." In every instance, you made happiness extrinsic to yourself. No wonder you are never happy. You are chasing mirages until death overtakes you.

But cynicism did not work, because in seeking pleasures you missed the joys of life. Pleasure is of the body; joy is of the mind and heart. Lobster Newberg gives pleasure to certain people, but not even the most avid lobster fans would ever say that it made them joyful. You can quickly become tired of pleasures, but you can never tire of joys. A pleasure can be increased to a point where it ceases to be a pleasure; it may even being to be a pain if carried beyond a certain point…But the joy of a good conscience, or the joy of a First Communion, or the discovery of truth, never turns to pain.

Furthermore, have you noticed that as your desire for pleasure increased, the satisfaction from the pleasure decreased? Do you think a philosophy of life is a right that is based in the law of diminishing returns?

You think you are having a good time, but time really is the greatest obstacle in the world to happiness, not only because it makes you take pleasures successively, but also because you are never really happy until you are unconscious of the passing of time. The more you look at the clock, the less happy you are. The more you enjoy yourself, the less conscious you are of the passing of time. You say, "Time passed like everything [else]." Maybe, therefore, your happiness has something to do with the eternal ...

Why are you disappointed? Because of the tremendous disproportion between your desires and your realizations. Your soul has a certain infinity about it, because it is spiritual. But your body, like the world about you, is material, limited, "cabined, cribbed, confined." You can imagine a mountain of gold, but you will never see one. In like manner, you look forward to some earthly pleasure, or position, or state in life, and once you attain it you begin to feel the tremendous disproportion between the ideal you imagined and the reality you possess. Disappointment follows. Every earthly ideal is lost by being possessed. The more material your ideal, the greater the disappointment; the more spiritual it is, the less the disillusionment.

Having discovered why you are disappointed, you take the next step of trying to avoid disappointments entirely. You ask yourself: "What do I desire above all things?" You want perfect life, and perfect truth, and perfect love. Nothing short of the Infinite satisfies you, and to ask you to be satisfied with less would be to destroy your nature. You want life, not for two more years, but always; you want to know all truths, not the truths of economics alone, to the exclusion of history. You also want love without end...

With your feet on earth, you dream of Heaven; creature of time, you despise it; flower of a day, you seek to eternalize yourself. Why do you want Life, Truth, Love unless you were made for them? How could you enjoy the fractions unless there were a whole? Where do they come from? Where is the source of light in the city street at noon? Not under autos, buses, nor the feet of trampling throngs, because their light is mingled with darkness. If you are to find the source of light you must go out to something that has no admixture of darkness or shadow; namely, to pure light, which is the sun. In like manner, if you are to find the source of Life, Truth, and Love, you must go out to a Life that is not mingled with its shadow, death; to a Truth not mingled with its shadow, error; and to a Love not mingled with its shadow, hate. You go out to something that is Pure Life, Pure Truth, Pure Love, and that is the definition of God. And the reason you have been disappointed is because you have not yet found Him!

It is God you are looking for. Your unhappiness is not due to your want of a fortune, or high position, or fame, or sufficient vitamins; it is due not to a want of something outside you, but to a want of something inside you. You cannot satisfy a soul with husks! If the sun could speak, it would say that it was happy when shining; if a pencil could speak, it would say that it was happy when writing--for these were the purposes for which they were made. You were made for perfect happiness. That is your purpose. No wonder everything short of God disappoints you.

But have you noticed that when you realize you were made for Perfect Happiness, how much less disappointing the pleasures of earth become? You cease expecting to get silk purses out of sows' ears. Once you realize that God is your end, you are not disappointed, for you put no more hope in things than they can bear. You cease looking for first-rate joys where there are only tenth-rate pleasures.

You begin to see that friendship, the joys of marriage, the thrill of possession, the sunset and the evening star, masterpieces of art and music, the gold and silver of earth, the industries and the comforts of life, are all gifts of God…He intended them to be bridges to cross over to Him [so that after] enjoying the good things of life you were to say: "If the spark of human love is so bright, then what must be the Flame!"

Unfortunately, many have become so enamored of the gifts the Great Giver of Life has dropped on the roadway of life that they build their cities around the gift, and forget the Giver. And when the gifts, out of loyalty to their Maker, fail to give them perfect happiness, they rebel against God and become cynical and disillusioned.

Change your entire point of view! Life is not a mockery. Disappointments are merely markers on the road of life, saying: "Perfect happiness is not here." Though your passions may have been satisfied, you were never satisfied, because while your passions can find satisfaction in this world, you cannot. Start with your own insufficiency and begin a search for perfection. Begin with your own emptiness and seek Him who can fill it.

Look at your heart. It tells the story of why you were made. It is not perfect in shape and contour, like a Valentine Heart. There seems to be a small piece missing out of the side of every human heart. That may be to symbolize a piece that was torn out of the Heart of Christ which embraced all humanity on the Cross. But I think the real meaning is that when God made your human heart, He found it so good and so lovable that He kept a small sample of it in Heaven. He sent the rest of it into this world to enjoy His gifts, and to use them as stepping stones back to Him, but to be ever mindful that you can never love anything in this world with your whole heart because you have not a whole heart with which to love. In order to love anyone with your whole heart, in order to be really peaceful, in order to be really wholehearted, you must go back again to God to recover the piece He has been keeping for your from all eternity.

--*You,* chapter 1

NOTES

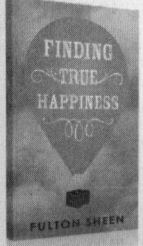

How many people do you know who could benefit from reading this book?

Visit **DynamicCatholic.com** and request SIX copies for just $18.

PHILOSOPHY OF PLEASURE

We all want happiness. We should all take the sensible step of learning that there are three laws of pleasure which, if followed, will make the attainment of happiness immeasurably easier.

The first law: *If you are ever to have a good time, you cannot plan your life to include nothing but good times.* Pleasure is like beauty; it is conditioned by contrast. Fireworks would not delight us if they were set off against a background of fire, or in the blaze of the noonday sun: they need to stand out against the darkness. Lilies bring us special pleasure because their petals rise, surprisingly, on the waters of foul ponds. Contrast is needed to help us see each thing being visibly itself.

Pleasure, by the same principle, is best enjoyed when it comes to us as a "treat," in contrast to experiences that are less pleasurable. We make a great mistake if we try to have all our nights party-nights. No one would enjoy Thanksgiving if every meal were a turkey dinner. New Year's Eve would not delight us if the whistles blew at midnight every night.

Fun rests on contrasts, and so does the enjoyment of a funny situation. If a bishop has a miter thrust on the side of his head by an errant master of ceremonies, it makes us laugh; it would not be funny if all bishops always wore their miters askew.

Our enjoyment of life is vastly increased if we follow the spiritual injunction to bring some mortification and self-denial into our lives. This practice saves us from being jaded; it preserves the tang and joy of living. The harp-strings of our lives are not thin, made slack by being pulled until they are out of tune; instead, we tighten them and help preserve their harmony.

Self-discipline brings back to us the excitement of our childhood, when our pleasures were rationed--when we got our dessert at the end of the meal and never at the start.

The second law: *Pleasure is deepened and enhanced when it has survived a moment of tedium or pain.* This law helps us to make our prized pleasures last for a whole lifetime. To do so, we must keep going at anything we do until we get our second wind. One enjoys a mountain-climb more after passing though the first moment of discouraged exhaustion. One becomes more interested in a job or work after the first impulse to drop it has been overcome.

In the same way, marriages become stable only after disillusionment has brought the honeymoon to an end. The great value of the marital vow is in keeping the couple together during the first quarrel; it tides them over their early period of resentment, until they get the second wind of true happiness at being together. Married joys, like all joys, are born out of some pain...the cross must be the prelude to the crown.

The third law: *Pleasure is a by-product, not a goal.* Happiness must be our bridesmaid, not our bride. Many people make the great mistake of aiming directly at pleasure; they forget that pleasure comes only from the fulfillment of a duty or obedience to a law--for man is made to obey the laws of his own nature as inescapably as he must obey the law of gravity. A boy has pleasure eating ice-cream because he is fulfilling one of the "oughts" of human nature: eating. If he eats more ice-cream than the laws of his body sanction, he will no longer get the pleasure he seeks, but the pain of a stomachache. To seek pleasure, regardless of law, is to miss it.

Shall we start with pleasure or end with it? There are two answers to the question: the Christian and the pagan. The Christian says, "Begin with the fast and end with the feast, and you will really savor it." The pagan says, "Begin with the feast and end with the morning-after headache."

--*Way to Happiness,* chapter 7

NOTES

Everybody Needs to Forgive Somebody
Allen R. Hunt

Get a FREE*copy at **DynamicCatholic.com**
Shipping and handling not included.

SILENCE

We live in the most talkative age in the history of the world. It would take ten or fifteen million men in previous ages to communicate to others the same information which one person today provides in a single broadcast. The love of noise and excitement in modern civilization is due in part to the fact that people are unhappy on the inside. Noise exteriorizes them, distracts them, and makes them forget their worries for the moment. There is an unmistakable connection between an empty life and a hectic pace. To make progress the world must have action, but it must also know *why* it is acting, and that requires thought, contemplation, and silence.

The world is in danger of becoming like a turnstile that is in everybody's way but stops nobody; it is a place where we look into everything but see nothing. Felix Frankfurter tells the effect of excessive talkativeness on government; everything is done under blare and noise, the deliberative process is impaired and government becomes too susceptible to quick thinking. It is, I believe, of deep significance that the Constitution of the United States was written behind closed doors, and it is well to remember that earth was thrown on the streets of Philadelphia to protect the convention from the noise of traffic. It might also be added that when the Apostles received the Holy Spirit it was behind closed doors too, and after they [had] kept nine days of silence awaiting the coming of heavenly Wisdom.

Action is the great need of the Eastern world; silence, the need of the Western. The East with its fatalism does not believe that man does anything; the West with its actionism believes that man does everything. Somewhere in between is the golden mean wherein silence prepares for action. He who holds his tongue for a day will speak much more wisely tomorrow. Even friendships are matured in silence. Friends are made by words; love is preserved in silence. The best friends are those who know how to keep the same silences. As Maeterlinck wrote: "Speech is too often not, as the Frenchman defined it, the art of concealing thought, but a quiet stifling and suspending thought, so that there is none to conceal…Speech is of time, silence of Eternity."

The ancient Spartans used to say that "a fool cannot be silent" and the Scriptures say that "a fool's voice is known by many words" (Ecclesiastes 5:2). It is all very well to plaster our church lawn with placards saying: "Leave the world better than you find it," but we will never leave the world better until, through silence, contemplation, and prayer we improve ourselves. We must leave the world to help the world. That life is most effectively lived which every now and then withdraws from the scene of action to contemplation, where one learns the terrible defeat and futility which come from excessive absorption in detail and action.

Throughout the United States there is growing what is known as the "Retreat Movement," in which busy men and women betake themselves over a weekend to a quiet place in the country, where they spend time in silence, prayer, and purging their consciences. The ancient Romans used to keep a bowl outside the business house, and whenever they left it at the close of the day, they washed their hands--as if to imply they even washed their hands of their business.

In silence, there is humility of spirit or what might be called "wise passivity." In such the ear is more important than the tongue. God speaks, but not in cyclones--only in the zephyrs and gentle breezes. As the scientist learns by sitting passively before nature, so the soul learns wisdom by being responsive to His Will. The scientist does not tell nature its laws; nature tells the scientist. We do not tell or impose our will on God; in silence like Mary, we await an Annunciation.

From this, learn the lesson that those who would become wise must become silent. A mirror is silent, yet it reflects forests, sunsets, flowers and faces. Great ascetic souls, given to years of meditation, have taken on a radiance and a beauty which are beyond the outlines of face. They seem to reflect, like the mirror on the outside, the Christ they bear within. What is really important is what happens within us, not outside us. The rapidity of communication, the hourly news broadcasts, tomorrow's news the night before--all these make people live on the surface of their souls. The result is that very few live inside themselves. They have their moods determined by the world. Instead of carrying their own atmosphere with them, as the earth does as it revolves around the sun, they are like barometers that register every change in the world outside. Silence alone can give them an inner sanctuary into which they may retire for repose, as hidden gardens wherein like Adam and Eve before the Fall they walk with God in the cool of evening.

Only in solitariness is true spirituality born, when the soul stands naked before its God. In that moment these are the only two realities in the universe. In this discovery is born love of neighbor, for then we love our fellow human beings, not because of what they can do for us, but because we see that they too are real or potential children of God. Though truth is not personal, we make it personal by contemplation.

---*Way to Inner Peace,* chapter 45

REPOSE

Never before have men possessed so many time-saving devices. Never before have they had so little time for leisure or repose. Yet few of them are aware of this: advertising has created in modern minds the false notion that leisure and not working are the same--that the more we are surrounded by bolts and wheels, switches and gadgets, the more time we have conquered for our own.

But this division of our days into working and not-working is too simple; in practice, for most men, it leaves out the very possibility of real leisure. They waste precious hours away from work in aimless loafing, in negative waiting-around for something interesting to come along.

True repose is not a mere intermission between the acts of the working-life. It is an intense activity, but of a different kind. Just as sleeping is not a cessation of life, but living of a different sort from wakefulness, so repose is an activity no less creative than that of our working hours.

Repose—true leisure—cannot be enjoyed without some recognition of the spiritual world, for the first purpose of repose is the contemplation of the good. Its goal is [one of] true perspective: the small incidents of everyday life in their relation to the larger goodness that surrounds us. Genesis tells us that after the creation of the world, *"God saw all that He had made, and found it very good"* (Genesis 1:31). Such contemplation of his work is natural to man, whenever he, too, is engaged in a creative task. The painter stands back from his canvas to see whether the details of the seascape are properly placed. True repose is such a standing back to survey the activities that fill our days.

We cannot get a real satisfaction out of our work unless we pause, frequently, to ask ourselves why we are doing it, and whether its purpose is one [of which] our minds wholeheartedly approve. Perhaps one of the reasons why so many of our economic and political projects miscarry is because they are in the hands of men with eyes so tightly glued to what they are doing that they never stop to question whether it should be done at all. Merely keeping busy, merely getting paid, can never satisfy man's need for creative work.

A job of any kind can be lifted up and given Divine purpose, if it is seen in the perspective of Eternity. The sweeping of a floor, the driving of a garbage-truck, the checking of a list of boxcar numbers--all these can be "made good" through a simple act of the will which directs them to the service of God. The simplest task can be given spiritual significance and made Divine.

If we direct our work towards God, we shall work better than we know. The admission of this fact is another of the tasks for which we need repose. Once a week, man, reposing from work, does well to come before his God to admit how much of what he did during the week was the work of his Creator; he can remind himself, then, that the material on which he labored came from other Hands, that the ideas he employed entered his mind from a higher Source, that the very energy which he employed was a gift of God.

In such a mood of true repose, the scientist will see that he himself was not the author of his research volume on nature's laws, but only its proofreader. It was God who wrote the book. In such repose, the teacher will confess that every truth he passed on to his students was a ray from the sun of Divine Wisdom. The cook who peels potatoes after such a period of repose will handle them as humble gifts of God Himself.

Repose allows us to contemplate the little things we do in their relationship to the vast things which alone can give them worth and meaning. It reminds us that all actions get their worth from God: "worship" means "admitting worth." To worship is to restore to our workaday life its true worth by setting it in its real relationship to God, Who is its end and ours.

Such worship is a form or repose--of an intensely active and creative contemplation of Divine things, from which we arise refreshed. The promise of Jesus in the Gospel of St. Matthew is still waiting for those who are willing to hear it: *"Come to me, all you who labored and are burdened, and I will give you rest"* (Matthew 11:28).

--*Way to Happiness,* chapter 9

NOTES

Jesus Shock
Peter Kreeft

Get a FREE*copy at **DynamicCatholic.com**
*Shipping and handling not included.

SELF-INFLATION

One of the celebrated portrait artists of the world once said that he never knew a person to sit for a portrait who did not constantly talk about himself. This may be explained psychologically as a desire to impress the artist with his greatness, in order that the artist might translate it onto the canvas. But it is more likely that the habit of egotism was already so deeply encrusted that self-praise was rather automatic; it showed itself in the Pullman car as well as in the studio.

Rich men perhaps more than others are the greatest boasters, though it may be unconscious. Confusing *having* with *being* they think that since they possess material greatness, therefore, they must necessarily be great. Such proud people are much more subject to worry and anxiety than those who are not proud, for every little trial registers very sharply through their morbidly sensitive skin.

Nothing has contributed so much to egotism, pride, conceit, swell-headedness, and braggadocio as the assumption that an "inferiority complex" is always wrong. If the failure to assert oneself, to push others aside in seeking the first places at table, is the mark of a psychological disease, then satanic pride is on the throne. Depreciation of the efforts of others, the swaggering playing out of a dream and an illusion, an excessive tenderness about any personal insults and a callousness toward the feeling of others become the daily behavior pattern.

The egotist, standing alone in his self-imagined greatness, lives in the world of a lie, because the truth about himself would puncture his self-inflation. Pride rightly has been called the source of all other evils. As the great poet put it "Fling away ambition; By that sin fell the angels; How can man, then, the image of his Maker, expect to win by it?" (Shakespeare, *Henry the Eighth,* Act III, Scene ii, Line 441).

A word hardly ever mentioned in modern speech is "humility," or the virtue which regulates a person's undue estimation of himself. Humility is not underestimating oneself, such as the talented singer denying that he can sing. Humility is truth, or seeing ourselves as we really are--not as we think we are, nor as the public believe us to be, or as our press notices describe us. If the candle compares itself with the lightning bug, it boasts of the greater light; but if compares itself with the sun, it sees itself but as its feeble ray. As the artist must judge his painting by the sitter, as the die maker must judge his coin by the model, so we must judge ourselves by our Maker and all that He intended us to be.

The humble are not cast down by the censures or the slights of others. If they have unconsciously given occasion for them, they amend their faults; if they deserve them not, they treat them as trifles. Humility also prevents putting an extravagant value on distinctions and honors. Praise will generally make the humble person uncomfortable, because he knows that whatever talents he has are gifts from God. He receives praise as the window receives light, not as the battery receives a current. The humble may be great, but if they possess that virtue, they hire no press agents, they blow no trumpets, they affect no mannerisms, they unfold no banners, they court no adulation, but while aiding and enlightening others, they long to be like the angels who, while ministering to others, are themselves unseen.

Humility is the pathway to knowledge. No scientist would ever learn the secrets of the atom if, in his conceit, he told the atom what he thought it ought to do. Knowledge comes only with humility before the object which can bring us truth.

In like manner, many minds today will not accept Revelation or faith because their pride has blocked the inflow of new knowledge. Only docile minds can receive new truth. Pride makes a person insoluble and, therefore, prevents his entering into amalgamation with others. Humility, on the contrary, because of its basic receptivity to the good of others, makes it possible to receive the joys of union with God. That is why Our Divine Lord suggested that university professors will have to become children to enter the kingdom of heaven; they must admit, like children, that God knows more than they do.

---*Way to Inner Peace,* chapter 35

NOTES

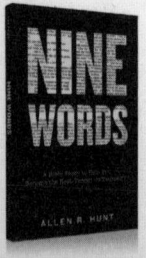

EGOTISM
THE ENEMY OF INNER PEACE

Here is a psychological suggestion for acquiring peace of soul. Never brag; never talk about yourself; never rush to first seats at table or in a theater; never lord it over others as if you were better than they.

These are but popular ways of expressing humility, which does not consist so much in humbling ourselves before others as it does in recognizing our own littleness in comparison to what we ought to be. The modern tendency is toward the affirmation of the ego, the exaltation of selfishness, riding roughshod over others in order to satisfy our own self-centeredness. It certainly has not produced much happiness, for the more the ego asserts itself, the more miserable it becomes.

Humility, which gives preference to others, is not very popular today principally because men have forgotten the Greatness of God. By expanding our puny little self to the Infinite, we have made the true Infinity of God seem trivial. The less knowledge we have of anything, the less significant it seems. Our hatred of a person often decreases as we learn to know him better. A boy graduating from high school is generally not as humble as when he graduates from medical school. At eighteen he thought he knew it all; at twenty-eight he feels himself ignorant in the face of the medical science he has yet to acquire. So it is with God. Because we do not pray or contemplate or love Him, we become vain and proud; but when we know Him better, we feel a deep sense of dependence which tempers our false independence. Pride is the child of ignorance, humility the offspring of knowledge.

Proud people think themselves to be better than they are, and when criticized always believe their neighbor is jealous or has a grudge against them. The humble know themselves as they really are, for they judge themselves as they judge time, by a standard outside themselves, namely, God and His Moral Law. The psychological reason for the modern fondness for news which deflates others or which brings out the evil in their lives, is to solace uneasy consciences which are already laden with guilt. By finding others who apparently are more evil than we, we falsely believe that we are somehow better "than the rest of men" (Luke 18:11). It used to be that the most popular biographies were stories about the lives of good men and women worthy of our imitation, rather than the recounting of scandals for the sake of making us believe we are more virtuous than we really are. The pagan Plutarch said: "The virtues of great men served me as a modern mirror in which I might adorn my own life."

Humility as it relates to others is a golden mean between blind reverence on the one hand and an overbearing insolence on the other. Humble people are not rigid exacters of things to which they have no undoubted right; they are always ready to overlook the faults of others, knowing that they have so many themselves. Neither are they greatly provoked at those sleights which put vain persons out of patience, knowing that as we show mercy to others, so shall we receive mercy from God.

Before undertaking a task great or small, before making decisions, before beginning a journey, the humble will acknowledge their dependence on God and will invoke His guidance and His blessing on all their enterprises. Even though they be placed above others by vocation, or by the will of the people, they will never cease to recognize that God has made of one blood all the nations that dwell on the earth. If they are very rich they will not be "defenders of the rights of the poor" without unloading their riches in their aid. Our modern world has produced a generation of rich politicians who talk love of the poor, but never prove it in action, and a brood of the poor whose hearts are filled with envy for the rich and covetousness of their money. The rich who are humble help, rather than use, the poor to pave their way to power.

Another evidence of want of humility is in regard to knowledge. Scripture bids us to be wise and "correctly interpret the word of truth" (2 Timothy 2:15). Humility moderates our estimate of what we know and will remind us that God gave to the wise more talents than others and more opportunities for developing those talents. But of him who has received much, much also will be expected. The intellectual leader has a tremendous responsibility upon him and woe to him if he uses his office of teaching to lead the young into error and conceit.

Notice how often today authors will have their picture taken with their book in their left hand, the title in full view to the camera, so that the photograph may tell the story: "Look Ma! My book 1." Television commentators have books on their desks with the title toward the audience so that the audience will be impressed. No one who reads books at a desk ever has the titles turned away--but toward himself. Perhaps some day when there are diaphanous walls, the intelligentsia will keep the titles on their bookshelves turned toward the wall so their next door neighbor will know how smart they are.

In the face of Divine Wisdom, all that we have, or do, or know, is a gift of God, and is only an insignificant molehill compared to His Mountain of Knowledge. Well indeed then may those who enjoy any relative superiority ask with St. Paul: "What do you have that you haven't received? And if you've received it, why do you boast as if it were yours alone?" (1 Corinthians 4:7).

--*Way to Inner Peace,* chapter 1

DESIRE

Desire is to the soul what gravitation is to matter. When we know our desires, we know the direction our soul is taking. If desire is heavenly, we go upwards. If it is wholly earthly, we go downwards. Desire is like raw material out of which we fashion either our virtues or vices. As Our Lord said: "Where your treasure is, there your heart is also" (Matthew 6:21).

Very few people ever withdraw enough from the world to ask themselves what is their basic desire. There are some who live a seemingly good life, who pay taxes, contribute to advertised welfare needs, but their basic desires are evil. Their goodness is often a want of opportunity for doing what is sinful. They are like the Elder Son in the Parable of the Prodigal Son who accuses his brother of "wasting his substance on harlots." There was nothing of this kind in the story. But the accusation revealed that the Elder Son would have done this very thing if he had been his brother.

On the other hand, there are some people who do very evil things, but who have a basic desire to be good, and are waiting for the day when a helpful hand will lift them from the pit. It was of such a group that Our Lord said: "Tax collectors and prostitutes are entering the Kingdom of God ahead of you [Scribes and Pharisees]" (Matthew 21:31).

Contentment depends upon the control of our desires. Advertising serves many needs, but it has also made luxuries appear as necessities, and created a desire for goods which the individual cannot possibly possess in their fullness. The Eastern World has struck on the secret of inner peace by suggesting that [it] is dependent on the control and limitation of desires. St. Paul said: "I have learned to be content with what I have" (Philemon 4:11). Contentment is not indifference, though the ignorant sometimes make that identification. Contentment does not mean immunity from trial, for it can know sighs and tears, but its feelings are never allowed to run into fretfulness. If it can not have what it wants, it never broods over its disappointments, but brightens them by sweet submission. It has no kinship with fatalism, which refuses to plan or act in the belief that nothing can be altered. It is such fatalism which characterizes certain Eastern philosophies and makes progress impossible. In contentment one does not submit before he has prayed and acted, but after one has done all he can, accepting the event as the will of the Lord.

There is a world of difference between submitting to the Divine Will from sullenness and submitting to it knowing that God is Supreme Wisdom, and that some day we will know all that happened, happened for the best. There is a marvelous peace that comes into the soul if all trials and disappointments, sorrows and pains are accepted either as deserved chastisement for our sins, or as a healthful discipline which will lead us to greater virtue. The violin strings, if they were conscious, would complain when the musician tightened them, but this is because they do not see that the sacrificial strain was necessary before they could produce a perfect melody. Evils actually become lighter by patient endurance, and benefits are poisoned by discontent.

Contentment is based on the idea that "our sufficiency is not from ourselves but from God" (2 Corinthians 3:5). The soul does not desire or lack more than what God has supplied him. His will suits his state after he has exhausted his resources and his desire does not exceed his power. Hence, everything that happens is judged to be as good and worthy of Divine appointment. As Socrates observed: "He is nearest to God who needs the fewest things."

Contentment is not inconsistent with our endeavor to have our condition improved. We do everything we can, as if all depended on us, but we trust in God as if everything depended on Him. The talents we have must be put to work, but if they yield only a certain return, we do not murmur because the return is not greater. When we really examine our consciences we have to admit that we have received more than we morally deserved! The discontent is far greater among the over-privileged than the underprivileged. The rich need the psychoanalysts more than the poor. Few European minds cracked under two wars. Many American minds have. The first learned not to expect anything. This is a lesson America has yet to learn.

--*Way To Inner Peace,* chapter 6

NOTES

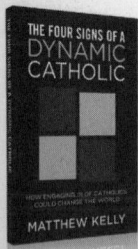

SADNESS

The wise man said: "Cast sadness far from thee, because it has killed many, and is good for nothing." There is hardly anything as apt to bring our hearts to a state of irksome disgust as sadness. Those who have made a psychological study of sadness tell us that one of its principal effects is to disturb our judgments, making us take a darker view of life than the facts justify. Thus, sadness leads to pessimism, and the reverse is also true--all pessimists are necessarily sad: disaster, for them, is just around the corner. A second effect of sadness is to make us rude to others and severe towards them, suspicious and ready to put the worst interpretation on the actions of everyone around us.

There are different ways of trying to overcome the sense of sadness. Some people take recourse to alcohol to make them forget. Others fling themselves into carnal pleasures hoping that the intensity of a momentary thrill will compensate them for want of a goal and a purpose in life. But all sad people are alike in this: at some time they say—perhaps scarcely conscious that they are saying it—"I do not love myself." This is not an "inferiority complex." It is rather the higher part of the self looking down on the lower part and reprimanding it for its pitiable condition. Animals cannot reflect on themselves as human beings do; hence they cannot feel the same kind of disgust.

There is a remedy for sadness--the one suggested by the Scriptures. To some minds it may seem farfetched when it says: "If you are suffering, pray!" (James 5:13) Actually, these words touch on a profound psychological truth, for they imply that we must be reconciled to ourselves in order to be happy. So long as we are merely the battleground of a war between the lower self and the higher self within us, there can be no relaxation and no joy. But to resolve the conflict, to bring the battle to an end, we must see ourselves as we really are. It does no good to blame the golf club if our game is at fault, or the pitcher because we spill the milk; the fault must be seen as our own in little mishaps of this kind, and for our states of mind as well. The discovery that we are to blame for being the way we are is greater than the discovery made by an explorer--such a discovery of our own fault is impossible unless there be a higher standard outside ourselves, from whose love we know that we have fallen.

When our own responsibility for our sadness has been faced, prayer next leads us on to hope, because it shows us the real basis for our discontent: the knowledge that we could be quite different from the way we are. As one writer put it: "I was told that I was the offspring of a father and a mother. I had thought that I was more." And one is more. The Savior said that each one of us is of more worth than the whole visible universe (cf. Matthew 10:31 and Luke 12:6).

We begin to act differently when we recognize the immensity of our possibilities. Our whole life changes then, like that of a farmer when he discovers oil on what he had previously believed to be just a poor farm. Prayer overcomes sadness by putting us in relation with the Eternal, and then the change occurs. Before, we had thought ourselves unloved by anyone; now, we know that we are loved by God.

Unless we put God between ourselves and our previous life, we cannot hope to make real spiritual progress. But God does not give Himself to us until we have begun to feel our own nothingness. By assenting to the poverty of our personality, we open the floodgates of Divine riches. It has been said that no one is a hero to his valet. It would be truer to say that no one is a hero to himself. Plutarch may tell us that Cato was a great human being; but to Cato, Cato was weak.

It is one thing to discover one's nothingness, and to rest there--that is sadness. It is quite another thing to discover that one is nothing, and from there to make use of the Divine Energies--that is joy. Mediocrity is a sin against ourselves, a kind of sacrilege. The *ennui* some hearts feel is nothing but the instinctive reaction of their great and undeveloped possibilities in the face of the triviality and mediocrity of their lives. All around us, birds are flying, musical in song, eager to enter into our souls. But until we are reconciled with the goal of life, they have to be content to perch on the top of our roof for a moment, and then fly away.

To pass from sadness to joy requires a birth, a moment of travail and labor, for no one ever mounts to a higher level of life without death to the lower. Before such an ascent, conscience, for a moment, has a hard, stern work to do. Pearls come from the bottom of the water, gold from the depths of the earth, and the great joys of life are to be found in the recesses of a contrite, broken heart.

Joy is the happiness of love—love aware of its own inner happiness. Pleasure comes from without, but joy comes from within, and it is, therefore, within the reach of everyone in the world. For if there is sadness in our hearts it is because there is not enough love. But to be loved, we must be lovable; to be lovable, we must be good; to be good, we must know Goodness, and to know Goodness is to love God, and neighbor, and everybody in the world.

---*Way to Inner Peace,* chapter 13

MOODS

Our Blessed Lord advised us: "When you fast, do not be sad or wear a long face as the hypocrites do" (Matthew 6:16). Then He cautioned His hearers to so dress themselves that no one would know they were fasting. Sadness is atheistic; it is not Christian. It is atheistic not only because it shows a lack of faith, leaving one with no *invisible* means of support, but also because it robs one of hope, as day adds to day, and the lease on life runs out. Many who have an empty stomach or a trial on the inside, placard it on their faces, register it in their voices and show it in their actions. Their disposition is either morose, taciturn, moody, grouchy, bitter or sharp. In a word, they are sad.

All has not gone well at the office or in the factory. The husband returns and answers his wife in monosyllables, if he answers her at all. The phone rings and a customer is at the other end; all is sweetness and light. This disproves those who say that bad humor is really not our fault at all, it is due to getting up on the wrong side of the bed, or "my rheumatism is bothering me today," or "my corn hurts and I know it is going to rain." These excuses are the same as those given in universities for sins, such as blaming it on our genes, or on society, or on the stars. The truth of the matter is, as Shakespeare says, "The fault ...is not in our stars, but in ourselves" (*Julius Caesar,* Act I, Scene ii, Line 134). External circumstances may condition our mental outlook and our dispositions, but they do not *cause* them.

Just as there is a right and wrong theory about the sun and the earth, so there is a right and wrong theory about external circumstances. If we revolve about what happens on the outside, then the latter determines our moods and attitudes. But if we make what is external revolve around us, we can determine the amount of their influence. Either what is outside makes our moods, or our moods determine our outlook on what is outside us. The pot that over-boils can boil over the temper, or the temper can see the pot over-boil and not get mad. Continuing that figure, it may be said that there are some people who in a quarrel, love to keep the "pot boiling."

Rainy days do make some people sad, but the author remembers saying once to a resident of Killarney: "Too bad it's raining." He answered: "But it's a good day to save your soul." Come to think about it, it may be easier to do that on rainy days than on sunny days. Our humor and disposition are not so much the reflection of the weather or the wrong side of the bed, as they are the reflections of the state of our soul. What is outside of us is beyond our control; but what is within us can be mastered and woven to any desired pattern. As Pascal once said: "Time and my moods have little relationship; I have my fogs and my bad weather within me." Our personal dispositions are as window panes through which we see the world either as rosy or dull. The way we color the glasses we wear is the way the world seems to us. To a great extent what we see is colored from the inside, rather than from the outside.

Two considerations are helpful in developing a good disposition. The first is to be mindful that a happy conscience makes a happy outlook on life, and an unhappy conscience makes us miserable on the inside and everyone else miserable on the outside.

When our conscience bothers us, whether we admit it or not, we often try to justify it by correcting others, or by finding fault with them. The readiness to believe evil about others is in large part ammunition for a thousand scandals in our own hearts. But by finding black spots in others, [we] believe they distract attention from [our] own miserable state. The good conscience, on the contrary, finds good in others even when there is some discontent with self.

The second aid to good humor is the spirit of joy. Joy is rejoicing in another's progress. This is one of the rarest virtues and the last to be won. Too often the progress of others is regarded as stolen from self. A man loses his good humor when he calls his wife "dear" when they are out and "ox" when at home. The wife loses her joy when she would rather spend her time mending his ways than mending his socks. All have joy when they thank God that their friends have done good work, that they are loved by others, and that their virtues proclaim the joy of a good conscience.

--*Way to Inner Peace,* chapter 15

NOTES

MENTAL CASES ARE INCREASING

Human beings have always taken for granted that there would be in their midst a few unfortunate individuals whose mental outlook would be warped and unpredictable. But what is disturbing today is the number of otherwise normal people who, in popular language, are "cracking up." Some are young, otherwise happily married; others are in middle life, with apparent security; but regardless of the age group, as a good American psychiatrist wrote, "Mental cases are the stepchild of modern civilization."

Leaving to the medical profession those who are suffering from functional and organic disturbances which affect the mind, our problem is to inquire into the reason for the many marginal or fringe cases of mental instability. Coming quickly to the point, it appears to be this: Our generation has been raised on the idea of "self-expression," which, being translated negatively, means there should never be any self-restraint. Every desire and impulse which satisfies the ego is considered good; any form of self-denial, or repression of biological urges, is considered as harmful to the personality. The ego is flattered and pampered, even to the point where children are raised on the theory that they should never be disciplined, much less punished or reprimanded for their selfishness.

When a person builds his philosophy of life on the principle of self-will, he is in for a tremendous shock. It happens that most other people he meets in the world have exactly the same principle. The result is that one individual has his self-will contradicted by another; the ego is negated by another ego; wishes are not fulfilled; whims are negated, crossed and rejected by other egos equally bent on self-assertion. This constant battering and challenge from other wills makes the mind confused; fills it with the sense of being persecuted; creates unhappiness, revenge and spitefulness.

Some seek professional advice regarding their confused mental state, and are told that they are suffering from an "inferiority complex." The truth of the matter is, nobody who is self-willed has an inferiority complex; he has a superiority complex. He is so full of conceit, pride and aggressive assertiveness that his hurt feelings may for the moment appear as inferiority. But he would not feel hurt if he did not have a diabolic pride, or superiority which would treat anyone who does not flatter him as Pontius Pilate treated Christ. Pilate washed his hands of Christ and had Him executed.

The hour has come for educators, sociologists and citizens to reverse their steps, to see that if the self is to be really happy, it must be disciplined, pruned, denied and negated by self. No better law for inner peace has ever been given than that of the Divine Savior: "If any one will come after me, let him take up his cross daily and follow me." (Luke 9:23). In other words, crosses and contradictions are a part of life. We are to expect them from others simply because they are often as unregenerate as ourselves. Contradictions from others will hurt us less when we have first contradicted ourselves. The hand that is calloused will not pain as much as a soft hand, on catching a hard ball. Contradictions can even be assimilated and used for further taming of our own errant impulses. But the will that always insists on having is own way, begins to hate its own way. Those who live only for self begin to hate self. Self is too narrow, confining and dark a sanctuary for happy adoration.

Crosses are inescapable. Those who start with self-love have already created for themselves the possibility of millions of other crosses from those who live by the same pride. But those who discipline themselves and tame the ego by little acts of self-denial have already prepared themselves to meet crosses from the outside; they have familiarized themselves with them, and the shock is less when they are thrust on their shoulders.

There are only two things we can do with crosses—carry them or kick against them. We can merge them in God's plan for life and thus make them serve our inner peace and happiness, or we can stumble over them to the glen of weeping. Selfishness is the cause of much mental sickness; otherness, sympathy, forgiveness and self-discipline are the cure.

---*Way to Inner Peace,* chapter 16

NOTES

LONELINESS

Dante begins one of his finest poems with: "At the midpoint of my life I came to the dark wood." By the dark wood, Dante meant that moment in middle age when one loses the zest for life.

Tolstoy, the great Russian writer, said that he passed through it: "It all took place at a time when so far as my outward circumstances went, I ought to have been completely happy. I had a good wife who loved me and whom I loved; good children and large property which was increasing with no pains on my part. I was more respected by my kinsfolk and acquaintances than I had ever been; I was loaded with praise by strangers; and without exaggeration I could leave my life already famous. Moreover, I was not insane or ill." He concludes by saying that life had lost all of its savor. He was lonely, until he found God.

On the level of ordinary life, there is perhaps more loneliness today than in any previous period of history. Children are lonely because they are teased, because of favoritism shown to others, because 5 million of them live in broken homes, or because their mothers are at work all day, returning at night to say as one mother did: "I had almost forgotten I had you."

Youths are lonely because they lack status; so they dress like one another in order to be part of the crowd. Unmarried people are lonely because they are torn between self-giving and self-sufficiency; many married people are lonely together, like ships that pass in the night.

The basic reason for loneliness is that man today has divorced himself from both love of God and love of neighbor. The peculiar characteristic about modern loneliness is that we can be in crowds and yet not be part of them. There is no loneliness like the loneliness of a big city.

It is a paradox that in an age when men are determined to love only self, they hate to be alone. Men used to live for society. Now, living for the ego, they cannot stand their ego. One wants to be the master of one's ego, but one is so lonely with it.

The intelligentsia are often more lonely than the simple people because, having a greater pride and independence, they become authoritarian and inconsiderate in dealing with others; this increases their loneliness. They do nothing to love neighbor, but they still want to be loved. And nothing creates a vacuum like wanting to be loved. To demand love is to lose love. A selfish heart creates its own vacuum.

Would not a violin, if it were endowed with consciousness, be lonely if it did not know why it was made? One such unhinged soul who had completely lost a sense of vocation and destiny and purpose in life wrote his own epitaph later to be inscribed on his tombstone: "Born a human person. Died a wholesale grocer."

Every woman is beautiful when she is loved. There are some who have no beauty in themselves, but they become beautiful in the eyes of the beloved. This is the way we are in relationship to God. We take on an inner glow with the consciousness that we are loved. A husband can be responsible for his wife's premature aging, in the sense that she loses the beauty with which the husband once endowed her when he loved her. A sinner feels somewhat the same way without the love of God. His soul aches, wrinkles and cracks; he has broken the bond of love. The moment he seeks to restore it, he becomes young again.

--*Walk With God,* chapter 35

NOTES

Ordinary Lives Extraordinary Mission
John R. Wood

Get a FREE* copy at **DynamicCatholic.com**
*Shipping and handling not included.

TRUTH
FORGOTTEN IDEAL

Submission is one of the deepest needs of the human heart. After a century-and-a-half of false liberalism, in which it was denied that anything was true, and that it makes no difference what you believe, the world reacted [through] totalitarianism. It grew tired of its freedom, just as children in progressive schools grow tired because of their license to do whatever they please. Freedom fatigues those who want to shirk responsibility. Then they look for some false god into whose hands they can throw themselves, so they will never have to think or make decisions for themselves. Nazism, Fascism, and Communism came into being during the twentieth century as a reaction against false liberalism.

Self-will always repudiates a truth which challenges it. However successful self-will may be, it is never satisfied; that is why the egotist is always critical. The "head that wears the crown is uneasy," not because he is tired of the crown, but because he is tired of himself. He has it within his power to do anything he pleases, and this living without boundaries and limitations becomes as dull and stagnant as a swamp. A river must be happier than a swamp because it has banks and boundaries; a swamp is a valley of liberty that has lost its shores and became "liberal."

The only ones who are really free from the bondage and the burden of self are those who hold to a truth. "The truth will make you free," said Our Divine Lord (John 8:32). Only the boxer who knows the truth about fighting is free to stay on his feet. Only the one who knows the truths of engineering is free to build a bridge that will stand. The lover of truth is under an eternal law of rectitude; as he submits to it, he enjoys peace.

Truth is not something we invent; if we do, it is a lie; rather, truth is something we discover, like love. In that great book of C.S. Lewis called *The Screwtape Letters,* there is a series of correspondence between an uncle devil in Hell and a young nephew devil on earth. The young devil is trying to win souls over to himself by talking about the "Truth of Materialism." The old devil reprimands him, saying that he must not talk about "truth"; that is the word that is used by "our enemy, God." You might confuse minds; get them to inquire whether a thing is "liberal or reactionary," "right or left," "modern or behind the times." Evidently Screwtape, the old devil, has succeeded pretty well with politicians and others.

Truth does not [change], but truth does develop. Two and two do not make four in the thirteenth century, and sixteen in the twentieth, but arithmetic does develop into geometry, and geometry into calculus. Nor is truth easy to discover, particularly when it affects our lives. There are two kinds of truth: speculative and practical. Speculative truth is the truth of knowing, such as comes to us from philosophy, mechanics, physics and chemistry. Practical truth, however, is concerned with doing and living, such as ethics and morals.

The first kind of truth is very easy to accept, e.g., London is the capital of England. The reason is because it does not in any way involve a change in our conduct. It makes no practical difference to our lives. But the truth of morality, such as purity, justice, prudence and charity are not so easy for acceptance, because they often demand a revolution in our behavior. That is why men are more willing to accept objections against a principle of morality than against a theory of science. Our Divine Lord referred to the difficulty of accepting practical truths when He said: "You will not come to me because your lives are evil" (cf. John 5:19-47).

Truth is a narrow path; either side is an abyss. It is easy to fall either to the right or to the left; it was easy to be an idealist in the nineteenth century, as it is easy to be a materialist in the twentieth century; but to avoid abysses and walk that narrow path of truth is as thrilling as a romance. Truth is like the veins of metal in the earth; it is often very thin and runs not in a continuous layer. If we lose it once, we may have to dig for miles to find it again. Grains of truth are like grains of gold that prospectors find; they can be discovered after a long search; they must be sifted from error with great patience; they must be buried with sacrifice to erase the dross and washed in the streams of honesty. Notice how often today men in public life accuse one another of "lying." Why is it they never speak of truth? May it not be that they studied in the same school as Pilate and asked, "What is Truth?" (John 18:38) and then turned their backs on it. It takes a heap of virtuous living for any one of us to discover Truth.

--Way to Inner Peace, chapter 36

NOTES

PATIENCE

The opposite of "flying off the handle" is *patience*—another virtue forgotten by our modern world, although Our Blessed Lord said: "By your patience you will save your souls" (Luke 21:19). The Greek origin of the word *patience* suggests two ideas: one continuance, the other submission. Combined, they mean submissive waiting, a frame of mind which is willing to wait because it knows it thus serves God and His Holy purposes.

A person who believes in nothing beyond this world is very impatient, because he has only a limited time in which to satisfy his many wants. The more materialistic a civilization is, the more it is in a hurry. Douglas Woodruff, the English essayist, said that "Americans do not like Rome; they heard it was not built in a day." The Chinese, on the other hand, can wait for centuries, for their wants are not compassed in a generation.

Patience is not something one is born with, it is something that is achieved, such as seeing. A baby has to learn to see—to distinguish objects, and learn distances. Sight is a gift of nature, but seeing has to be won. When Our Lord healed the blind man, he had to learn how to see, for he said that to him "men looked like trees walking" (Mark 8:24). So it is with self-possession and patience, but such a virtue is developed by resistance and control. The big problem all of us have to face is whether we will, under difficulties, ride out the storm to port. Of course, if we do not know *why* we are living, then we must substitute tiny little wishes for one great consuming purpose; and this makes life miserable and unhappy.

To us, often, the principal thing is the frustration, the war, the dislocation, the chaos, and the confusion. But patience ought to be the guiding virtue of the soul in the midst of this "confusion worse confounded." The winning of the battle of life is nothing but the winning of our souls, and souls are won by patience under tribulation.

Patience is not a virtue to be practiced only by the sick and by those in prison. Actually, few virtues are more essential for peace of soul, for there are hardly any circumstances of life where it cannot be practiced. There are four great areas of life in which patience can be learned. *First*, in the midst of provocations—that is, the indifference of others, the incivility and haughtiness of those with whom we work, the vexations at home, in the office, and on the highway. One of the reasons why people who are calm at home are impatient behind the steering wheel is because they know, as they shout at other drivers, that they are unknown. They regard anonymity as a shield for their character. *Second*, in disappointments—the rain on the day of the picnic, the late dinner guest, the cancelled visit, and the honor that never came through, test us. Giving way to violence under these circumstances is a loss of self-possession. *Third*, restraints. No one can always be his or her own master. The tin can that will not open, the key that will not turn, the zipper that refuses to zip—all these are circumstances under which losing one's temper is to lose inner calm. It does no good to blame the club when the golfer is at fault. To be impatient is to aggravate the evils we must endure, and thus postpone their solution. *Fourth*, injuries and wrongs. No station is so high as to be immune from unjust criticism. The higher we climb, the better the target we make for sticks and stones. It is well to remember under such circumstances what Walter Winchell once said: "No man will ever get ahead of you as long as he is kicking you in the seat of your pants."

There are many who excuse themselves, saying that if they were in other circumstances they would be much more patient. This is a grave mistake, for it assumes that virtue is a matter of geography, and not of moral effort. It makes little difference where we are; it all depends on what we are thinking about. What happens to us is not so important, but rather how we react to what happens. Judas and Peter both sinned against the Lord, and He called them both devils. But one became a Saint, because he overcame his weakness with the help of God's grace.

It is the winds and the winters which try the herbs, the flowers, and the trees, and only the strongest survive. So tribulation tries the soul, and in the strong it develops patience, and patience, in its turn, hope, and hope finally begets love.

Patience is the great remedy against becoming panicky. To be able to use reason and good judgment when everyone else goes to pieces not only saves self, but also neighbor. Men use reason better when they are calm, women use reason best at the point where man loses it. Passion impairs reason in a man; in a woman it does not. But, regardless of these differences, the patient soul can use judgment and counsel when all others are agitated and disturbed. Patience is power…the yoke sits easiest on the neck of the patient ox, and he feels his chain the lightest who does not drag, but carries it.

--Way to Inner Peace, chapter 40

NOTES

CONTENTMENT

Contentment is not an innate virtue. It is acquired through great resolution and diligence in conquering unruly desires; hence it is an art which few study. Because there are millions of discontented souls in the world today, it might be helpful for them to analyze the four main causes of discontent, and to suggest means to contentment.

The principle cause of discontent is *egotism*, or selfishness, which sets the self up as a primary plant around which everyone else must revolve. The second cause of discontent is *envy*, which makes us regard the possessions and the talents of others as if they were stolen from us. The third cause is *covetousness*, or an inordinate desire to have more, in order to compensate for the emptiness of our heart. The fourth cause of discontent is *jealousy*, which is sometimes occasioned through melancholia and sadness, and at other times by hatred of those who have what we wish for ourselves.

One of the greatest mistakes is to think that contentment comes from something outside us rather than from a quality of the soul. There was once a boy who only wanted a marble; when he had a marble, he only wanted a ball; when he had a ball, he only wanted a top; when he had a top, he only wanted a kite, and when he had the marble, the ball, the top, and the kite, he still was not happy. Trying to make a discontented person happy is like trying to fill a sieve with water. However much you pour into it, it runs out too rapidly for you to catch up.

Nor is contentment to be found in an exchange of places. There are some who believe that if they were in a different part of the earth, they would have a greater peace of soul. A goldfish in a globe of water, and a canary in a cage, on a hot day, began talking. The fish said: "I wish I could swing like that canary; I'd like to be up there in that cage." And the canary said: "Oh, how nice to be down in that cool water where the fish is." Suddenly a voice said: "Canary, go down to the water! Fish, go up to the cage!" Immediately they changed places, but neither was happy, because God originally had given each a place according to his ability, one that best suited his own nature.

The condition of our contentment is to be contained, to recognize limits. Whatever is within limits is likely to be quiet. A walled garden is one of the quietest places in the world; the world is shut out, and through its gates one can look upon it with the affection of distance, borrowing enchantment from it. So, if the soul of man is kept within limits (that is to say, not avaricious, greedy, over-reaching, or selfish), it, too, is shut into a calm, quiet, sunny contentment. Contented man, limited and bound by circumstances, makes those very limits the cure of his restlessness. It is not to the point whether a garden has one acre or three, or whether it has a wall; what matters is that we shall live within its bounds, whether they be large or small, in order that we can possess a quiet spirit and a happy heart.

Contentment, therefore, comes in part from *faith*—that is, from knowing the purpose of life and being assured that whatever the trials are, they come from the hand of a loving Father. Secondly, in order to have contentment, one must also have a *good conscience*. If the inner self is unhappy because of moral failures and unatoned guilt, then nothing external can give rest to the spirit. A third and final need is *mortification of desires,* the limitation of delights. What we over-love, we often over-grieve. Contentment enhances our enjoyment and diminishes our misery. All evils become lighter if we endure them patiently, but the greatest benefits can be poisoned by discontent. The miseries of life are sufficiently deep and extensive, without our adding to them unnecessarily.

Contentment with our worldly condition is not inconsistent with the desire for betterment. To the poorest man, Christianity says not to be merely content, but "be diligent in business." The contentment enjoined is for the time being. Man is poor today, and for this day, faith enjoins him to be satisfied; but deliverance from his poverty may be best for tomorrow, and therefore the poor man works for his increased prosperity. He may not succeed; if his poverty continues for another day, he accepts it, and then proceeds until relief comes. Thus, contentment is relative to our present state, and is not absolute in respect to the entire demands of our nature. A contented man is never [really] poor though he may have very, very little. The discontented man is never rich, let him have so very much.

--*Way to Happiness*, chapter 1

NOTES

Made for More
Curtis Martin

Get a FREE*copy at **DynamicCatholic.com**
*Shipping and handling not included.

JOY

Joy is the delightful experience of the feelings of pleasure at a good gained and actually enjoyed, or the prospect of good which one has a reasonable hope of obtaining. There can be both natural joys and spiritual joys. Natural joys would be the joy of youth before disappointment has stretched the soul, or the joy of health when food is pleasant and sweet, or the joy of success when the battle has been won, or the joys of affection when the heart is loved. All these natural joys are intensified by spiritual joys and put upon a more enduring basis. No earthly happiness would be thorough if it were not associated with a good conscience.

Spiritual joy is a serenity of temper in the midst of the changes of life, such as a mountain has when a storm breaks over it. To a man who has never rooted the soul in the Divine, every trouble exaggerates itself. He cannot put his full powers to any one thing because he is troubled about many things.

Joy is not the same as levity. Levity is an act; joy, a habit. Mirth is like a meteor, cheerfulness like a star; mirth is like crackling thorns, joy like a fire. Joy, being more permanent, makes difficult actions easier. Soldiers after a long day's march would hardly walk as nimbly as they do, if they did not march to music. A cheerful heart always finds a yoke easy and a burden light.

Certainly no nurse is helpful in a sick room unless she has the spirit of cheerfulness. Every nurse really ought to have two things before she enters a sick room: an incision and a sense of humor. An incision in order that she may know the value of pain; a sense of humor in order that she may know how to diffuse happiness. This incision need not be physical, but it should at least be symbolic, in the sense that there should be a deep appreciation of the woes and sufferings of others. There is nothing that so much adds to the longevity of sickness as a long face.

Joy has much more to do with the affections than with reason. To the man with a family, his wife and children call out and sustain his delights much more than his intellect could ever stimulate. Standing before a cradle, a father seems face to face with the attributes of an everlasting Being Who has infused His tenderness and love into the Babe. The power of rejoicing is always a fair test of a man's moral condition. No man can be happy on the outside who is already unhappy on the inside. If a sense of guilt weighs down the soul, no amount of pleasure on the outside can compensate for the loss of joy on the inside. As sorrow is attendant on sin, so joy is the companion of holiness.

Joy can be felt in both prosperity and adversity. In prosperity it exists not in the goods we enjoy, but in those we hope for; not in the pleasures we experience, but in the promise of those which we believe without our seeing. Riches may abound, but those for which we hope are the kind which moths do not eat, rust consume, nor thieves break through and steal. Even in adversity there can be joy in the assurance that the Divine Master Himself died through the Cross as the condition of His Resurrection.

If joy be uncommon today, it is because there are timid souls who have not the courage to forget themselves and to make sacrifices for their neighbor, or else because the narrower sympathies make the brighter things of the world to come, appear as vanities. As the pull from the belief in God and the salvation of the soul fade from life, so also joy vanishes and one returns to the despair of the heathens. The old Greeks and Romans always saw a shadow across their path and a skeleton at their feet...A famous Greek poet once said of life that it was better not to be born, and the next best thing was to quit life as soon as possible. All this is at the other extreme of St. Paul, who said: "Rejoice in the Lord always; again I say Rejoice!" (Philemon 4:4).

--*Way to Happiness,* chapter 3

NOTES

THE WILL
THE SECRET OF SANCTITY

There is one thing in the world that is definitely and absolutely your own, and that is your will. Health, power, life, and honor can all be snatched from you, but your will is irrevocably your own, even in Hell. Hence, nothing really matters in life, except what you do with your will. It is the drama of will which makes the story of the two thieves crucified on either side of Our Lord one of the absorbing incidents of history.

Both thieves at first blasphemed. There was no such thing as the good thief at the beginning of the Crucifixion. But when the thief on the right heard that Man on the Central Cross forgive His executioners, he had a change of soul. He began to accept his sorrows. He took up his cross as a yoke rather than as a gibbet, abandoned himself to God's will, and turning to the rebellious thief on the left, said: "Have you no fear of God, seeing that you are under the same condemnation! And we indeed justly, for the sentence we received corresponds to our crimes; but this man has done nothing wrong." Then from his heart, already so full of surrender to his Savior, there came this plea: "Remember me when you come into your kingdom." Immediately there came the answer of the Lord: "Amen, I say to you, this day you shall be with me in Paradise" (Luke 23:40-43).

Each of us, too, has a cross. Our Lord said: "If anyone would be my disciple, he must deny himself, and take up his cross, and follow me" (Mark 8:34). He did not say: "Take up My Cross." His Cross is not the same as yours, and yours is not the same as mine. Every cross in the world is tailor-made, custom-built, patterned to fit its bearer and no one else...

Our Lord deals separately with each of our souls. The crown of gold you want may have underneath it a crown of thorns, but the heroes who choose the crown of thorns, often find underneath it a crown of gold. Even those that seem to be without a cross actually have one. No one would have suspected that when Mary resigned herself to God's will by accepting the honor of becoming the Mother of God, she would ever have to bear a cross. It would seem, too, that one preserved free from original sin should be dispensed from the penalties of that sin, such as pain. And yet this honor brought her seven crosses and ended by making her the Queen of Martyrs.

There are, therefore, as many kinds of crosses as there are persons: crosses of grief and sorrow, crosses of want, crosses of abuse, crosses of wounded love, and crosses of defeat...

It is only when a log is thrown into the fire that it begins to sing. It was only when the thief was thrown into the fire of a cross that he found God. It is only in pain that some discover Love...

There will be a bright jewel of merit for those who suffer in this world. Because we live in a world where position is determined economically, we forget that in God's world the royalty are those who do His will. Heaven will be a complete reversal of the values of earth. The first shall be last and the last first, for God is no respecter of persons.

A wealthy and socially important woman went to Heaven. St. Peter pointed to a beautiful mansion and said, "This is your chauffeur's home." "Well," said she, "if that is his home, think what mine will be like." Pointing to a tiny cottage, Peter said, "There is yours." "I can't live like that," she answered. And Peter said, "I'm sorry, that is the best I could do with the material you sent up to me." Those who suffer as the good thief did, have sent ahead some fine material…

It is typically American to feel that we are not doing anything unless we are doing something big. But from the Christian point of view, there is no one thing that is bigger than any other thing. The bigness comes from the way our wills utilize things. Hence, mopping an office for the love of God is "bigger" than running the office for the love of money.

Each of us is to praise and love God in his own way. The bird praises God by singing, the flower by blooming, the clouds with their rain, the sun with its light, the moon with its reflection, and each of us by our patient resignation to the trials of our state in life.

If the gold in the bowels of the earth did not say *Fiat* to the miner and the goldsmith, it would never become the chalice at the altar; if the pencil did not say *Fiat* to the hand of the writer, we would never have the poem. If Our Lady did not say *Fiat* to the angel, she would never have become the House of God; if Our Lord did not say *Fiat* to the Father's will in Gethsemane, we would never have been redeemed; if the thief did not say *Fiat* in his heart, he never would have been the escort for the Master into Paradise.

The reason most of us are what we are--mediocre Christians, "up" one day, "down" the next--is simply because we refuse to let

God work on us. As crude marble, we rebel against the hand of the Sculptor, as unvarnished canvas, we shrink from the oils and tints of the Heavenly Artist. We are so "fearful lest having Him we may have naught else beside," forgetful that if we have the fire of Love, why worry about the sparks, and if we have the perfect round, why trouble ourselves with the arc. We always make the fatal mistake of thinking that it is what we do that matters, when really what matters is what we let God do to us. God sent the angel to Mary, not to ask her to do something, but to let something be done.

Since God is a better artisan than you, the more you abandon yourself to Him, the happier He can make you. It is well to be a self-made man, but it is better to be a God-made man. Try it—I mean you, whether you be Jew, Protestant, or Catholic—by spending a Holy Hour a day in prayer and mediation. Catholics should include morning Mass in their Hour, thus taking advantage of Calvary's sacrifice, in a world of lesser Calvaries.

God will love you, of course, even though you do not love Him, but remember, if you give Him only half your heart, He can make you only 50% happy.

You have freedom only to give it away. To whom do you give yours? You give it either to the moods, to the hour, to your egotism, to creatures, or to God.

Do you know that, if you give your freedom to God, in Heaven you will have no freedom of choice, because once you possess the Perfect, there is nothing left to choose; and still you will be perfectly free, because you will be one with Him whose heart is Freedom and Love.

--*You,* chapter 13

BIBLIOGRAPHY

Sheen, Fulton J. *Way to Happiness.* New York: Society of St. Paul/ Alba House, 1998.

Sheen, Fulton J. *Way to Inner Peace.* New York: Society of St. Paul/ Alba House, 1995.

Sheen, Fulton J. *Walk With God.* New York: Society of St. Paul/ Alba House, 2008.

Sheen, Fulton J. *You.* New York: Society of St. Paul/Alba House, 2003.